Twilight

Megan Shaughnessy Masten

authorHOUSE®

AuthorHouse™
1663 Liberty Drive, Suite 200
Bloomington, IN 47403
www.authorhouse.com
Phone: 1-800-839-8640

First published by AuthorHouse 9/17/2007

ISBN: 978-1-4343-2908-0 (sc)

Library of Congress Control Number: 2007906682

Printed in the United States of America
Bloomington, Indiana

This book is printed on acid-free paper.

For Dad, who understands.

WRITTEN POETRY

VISUAL POETRY

PROMISE

TWILIGHT

Look past the year as it slips and slows to meaning
Until you can't taste where it came from anymore
Savor the honey of things to be and smile

ANTICIPATION

Her fingers tremble as she fumbles with the zipper of the makeup bag, denting the silver polish. It's an eternity before her smoky eyes are done. She carefully applies the lavender lipstick then steps back to look at the final product. Heels break the overwhelming silence as they click on the tile and startle her. Her hips are too big, and her hair has already started to frizz out despite the many coats of hair spray. Her chest is flat and while her stomach protrudes. But the dress brings attention to her "Ojos Bonitos" and she says aloud, "I guess I look alright."

Driving to The Fireside Inn, she tells herself that she looks gorgeous tonight, and of course he will dance with her. She mentally repeats these things to herself until she almost believes them. She begins mouthing the words to songs that fill her mind's internal radio.

The headlights shine on the white sign. She checks the meter and speeds up. Leaning over, she slides the lever to turn the heat up. She eases to a stop at the sign, looks around, and moves forward.

You know, I wanted to be you but I'm only me, myself and jealousy doesn't make amends The world just keeps on spinning and soon I'll see her love lives on forever inside of you and me

She brakes, flips the turn signal on, and enters the overcrowded parking lot. She snaps her purse open and drops the key in, clinking against her "just in case" quarters. She reminds herself again that she is pretty before stepping onto the blacktop. Halfway across the parking lot she realizes she forgot to turn the headlights off. Turning slightly pink, she hurries back. She fumbles with the lock, leans into the car, and, cursing as a cold wind lifts her skirt, turns the lights off. She is shaking once again. *Calm down, girl. Everyone has done that.*

Walking past the smokers, she pushes the lobby door open, leaving fingerprints on the glass. All the guys are staring at the girl in front of her whose slitted dress showcases her hips. The table guarding the entrance boasts signs for ticket numbers. She opens her purse, takes the slip of paper out and joins the middle line. Her algebra teacher grabs the ticket without looking up, and runs a finger down his list until he finds the number. He recognizes her name and looks up: "You look very nice."

"Thank you," she breathes as she looks into the dimly lit room blinking with cameras flashes and girls squealing, "Oh-my-god I love your dress!" She walks to the doorway, holding her hand out for the stamp.

Taking a deep breath, she steps through.

YAWN

Somebody shot me last night
three times in the mouth
with a shiny metallic pistol.
Half an intake of breath to anticipate it
was not enough time to tongue the barrel.
PopPopPop all in a row
and I wondered if one was mine
and the other two got the children
until my lips closed on steel.
My throat was open,
wide as a yawn, sore as strep.
I didn't want to open
the eyes I didn't remember closing.
Later, -How is time measured
between consciousness'? -
I stayed silent, perched and waiting
but still unable or unwilling to move.

Haunted

I awake

squirming in the night

sensations vivid

inescapable

BECOMING A
WOMAN

Mother pinned her down tight
And cut delicate skin through the flood
No girl child could fight
That rusty tin lid crusted with blood

The elders who mutilated today
Closed her small and removed the clit
Commanded daughters mated to obey
Women all now chained and slit

SALLY

Princess in a house of Cowboys and Indians,
I waited and watched them shoot and wrestle
From the safety of the stuffed animal pile.
I held a polar bear, stroked her white fur,
Flicked my nails against the stiff eyes.
"Sweetheart, if you can name her she's yours."
Sally was mine as quick as that
And I held her tenderly without flicking
As I waited to hear the news.
"It's time to go home and meet your baby sister."
And our bear teeth smiles giggled.

ESTEY'S SONG

January baby, I named you Jesus.
A gift to me when I was four.
I'd play with my real dolly
With a gurgle, giggle and roar.

As playmates we argued constantly,
Tickle-attacking and biting.
Both of us were told to be the bigger one;
Just stop yelling and fighting.

I wanted to be like you:
Cheerleader, pianist, with many friends.
But I'm not. I'm me, myself, and
Jealousy doesn't make amends.

I left for college and then LA
But never forgot my sister.
We've been through a lot:
Mom's death and how we miss her.

Little sister? Not anymore;
Womanhood is calling. It's true.
Whatever happens remember one thing:
I'll always be here for you.

IF...

This plague would not be so horrid

if my memory were dim.

Or perhaps it would worsen

and I'd be lost forever to the sin.

LONG WALK HOME

Pale curvaceous pearl
Hush hush hush hush
No longer hers but his breasts
The rattle rattle of her chains

Hush hush hush hush
Vanity gone sour
The rattle rattle of her chains
Each time is unique

Vanity gone sour
Pretty pretty baby kitty
Each time is unique
Satisfied moan

Pretty pretty baby kitty
Click curtsey twirl
Satisfied moan
Only the tremble suggests

Click curtsey twirl
Crimson velvet crush
Only the tremble suggests
Why does she contain

Crimson velvet crush
Wilting this delicate flower
Why does she contain
Find search seek

Wilting this delicate flower
Cold concrete city
Find search seek
Home home home home

Cold concrete city
Push topple rush
Home home home home
Self rescued girl

Push topple rush
His frenzied quest
Self rescued girl
Uncontained

His frenzied quest
Have you seen this pretty
Uncontained
A model's physique

Have you seen this pretty
She is nearly grown
A model's physique
Chiming chiming the clock tower

She is nearly grown
Bruises heal beneath the blush
Chiming chiming the clock tower
Kneeling in the gutter to hurl

Bruises heal beneath the blush
Will anyone notice the stain
Kneeling in the gutter to hurl
Shaking clothes on bone

Will anyone notice the stain
Squinting through the bleak
Shaking clothes on bone
Noticing the committee

Squinting through the bleak
Triumphant rest
Noticing the committee
Who saves the weak

Triumphant rest
Stinging sorrow gush
Who saves the weak
Remain remain remain

BLISS

BLESSING

You have one of those faces
Where people, when they see you,
They get happy.

NICE JAMMIES

Enh... Eeennhh... Eeeeennnnhhhhh!!!
Groaning, he rolls over, slaps the alarm clock,
and slides out of bed. He saunters out of
his dorm room to hear, "Umm... I think maybe..."
Confused, he follows her gaze.
"I gotta pee," he explains, blushing.

SMILE

smile
blinding toothy
singing chewing giggling
sit by me
grin

No and Yes

Playful kissing innocent and sweet soft lips gently
Part warm tongues meet and slowly start to dance
With searching hands unclasping caressing
Her back down her spine sending chills
That linger as he turns her around and lifts
Her shirt while breathing I love you and in
Her mind she secretly begs him to make her
Tonight he circles her breasts her wobbly knees
Give out he guides her to the bed and takes off
Her jeans her silky white panties his boots and
Class ring as she lies there watching trembling
Slowly unbuttons his shirt and pants sliding them
Off his limbs intertwine with hers as he pushes two
Fingers inside her deep and soaking and
Pulsing he wiggles them back and forth in
Out in nibbling on her ear breathing rapid hot
Baby so hot encircling her holding her close so
Close now he pulls away and hovers above
Her licking her nibbling and tasting her
Sweetness he inches up his kiss lingering
On her thighs her belly her neck her nose

Their eyes meet and she is frightened
By his cloudy greedy gaze that does not see
Her body starts to dry up and chill and still he
Sucks her neck, her nipples as
He pushes into her no
No please I'm scared
Baby I love you I'm almost there
Honey you're so hot Ooooohh
Ouch you're hurting me
Stop that you're ruining it lie still
PLEASE STOP
Baby you know I love you ooohh you're so tight
No no no no no no no no no no

If you weren't so sexy I wouldn't
Have done that why did you make me
Hurt you you're a fucking tease
Look what you've done get out of here

INFINITE

Sweet baby don't cry,
Silence your fears.
I know it feels like
You're there and I'm here.

Sweet baby don't cry,
Bite your bottom lip.
You're not alone,
Not even for a pip.

Sweet baby don't cry,
Can you feel
My hand in yours?
The heat is real.

Sweet baby don't cry,
Start to sway.
Our blissful dance
Won't go away.

Sweet baby don't cry,
Meet my soft kiss.
Remember to breathe.
Do you long for this?

Sweet baby don't cry,
Whisper to the moon.
She sings of your love
Here in my room.

Sweet baby don't cry,
Close your damp eyes.
Through infinite space
Together we fly.

PAIN

His room
Was their room
Until he said no

Now she takes his knife
The one still holding his pain
And stretches forth her wrist
Lingering over the bowl
That's waiting
Expecting

It won't slice
She can't do it
Trembling icy shivers
Can't stop sobbing

Help me.

REMEMBER THIS

I could tell you, sweet young one,
and you would hear
but not understand
until it happens to you, my dear.
Even so, you did ask
and it wouldn't be polite
for me to walk away
leaving you answerless tonight.

Your time will come. I know this is so.
Your heart will fill with gladness
and then the agony of letting him go.
After it ends and all is night,
in that despair you'll see
the choice to shackle your worth to him
or set yourself free.

So remember my words child.
This is the core. You love you first
and then be ready for more.

FIRST KISS

I stand here shifting my weight foot to foot
Moths attack the hovering porch lamp
Trembling in the evening air
I had a great time tonight
Yeah let's do it again
Grinning he moves in
Shuffling closer
Leaning in
Relax
Kiss

I Know This Place

dragged out of normalcy my head bumps
on each step of the winding stairwell
quivering in invisible barbed wire shackles
searing freezing burns
my parched withered popping soul
and I am trapped in this impenetrable shadow
where the murderous solitude shrieks silence

LOOM

PUBERTY

Alex turned thirteen today and I went
to her murder mystery party.
There were too many kids there
so I had to share a character with Katie.
We were Burt the football star
trying to discover who murdered our teacher.
It was okay. I was really miserable
when I saw the great presents
everybody else gave Alex.
My small journal was so insignificant
compared to their stuff.
I was ninety-five percent certain she'd like it
when I picked it out, but failed anyway
and looked like a total geek in front of everybody.
I nearly started crying right there.
Half a character, worst present,
I should have stayed home.

HAZING

There's a game tomorrow
my squadmate had said
So I put my uniform on
when I crawled out of bed
Short skirt and bloomies
got smirks from my roomies
Then when the bus came
teammates called me insane
I'd worn mine
but it wasn't the time

Beaten

I didn't know what else to do to stop the pain,
so I sat there on my bedroom floor
and pummeled my legs.
My fists hit the inside of my thighs,
knees and shins, everywhere they could reach
on my pretzeled up legs.
The punches started slowly and forcefully
then escalated to madness;
I was punching anything
and everything I could reach...
my chest, arms, stomach, and legs
would all show the marks of my attack
for days afterwards.

It frightened me to have such strong feelings.
For nearly a year I had been suppressing them,
frightened of what monsters might come forth
if I let them. The moment I knew Mom was dead
I decided that I would take over,
carry on where she had left off.
I would raise my infant brother,
protect my sister, make sure Dad survived.
My needs and desires would be ignored.
I was fourteen years old.

I had two lives.
One was of a high school student:
school, boys, friends, homework, and rebellion.
The other was of an adult:
babysitting, motherhood, protecting, and giving.
It was emotionally exhausting living this way
and sometimes I couldn't hold back
those evil feelings.

Dad confronted me
after learning that I was failing math.
He always taught me that girls

can be just as good at "boy classes" as guys;
that women are not inferior in any way .
He maintained that I was smart.
He did not understand why I was failing a subject
that I had previously been put in gifted classes for.
Our discussion of sorts got way out of hand
and ended with me screaming at him
to leave me alone.

I stomped up the stairs and slammed my door,
then proceeded to hit myself.
I wanted to regain control and this was
the only way I could think of at that moment.
Maybe physical punishment would help.
I was so frustrated with myself
for having screamed at him,
or having felt anything negative at all.
I realized when I got to my room
that I was not mad at him
for looking into my school-work.
I was angry that he was butting into my life
when that was supposed to be Mom's job.
I guess what it comes down to is
I hated him for being alive when she wasn't.

When I slammed my door,
the vibrations knocked one of the photographs
off of the wall in the hallway.
Dad came in to scold me for shutting it so hard
and caught me hurting myself.
He stood there in the doorway, horrified
and speechless for a moment…
and then asked, "Why are you doing that?"
I didn't know, so I just stopped
and walked to the bed,
burying my tear-streaked face in my pillow.
He stood there for a few minutes
and then softly closed the door.

TANTRUM

I am not a child thrashing on the floor
or biting my sister's arm
as she tries to bar the door.

I am not a man slashing open my veins
or cursing incessantly
while driving in the flooding rains.

I am not an infant spitting up all I eat
or screaming inconsolably
for the seventh night this week.

I am not a woman starving myself slim
or weeping for months
at the mere thought of him.

I am not a teenager getting drunk and high
or living in silence
as friends choose to die.

I am not who I am.

WHERE IS THE HOPE?

When is it going to end? First

Her. Chose to kill it, the bitch.

Everyone advises me. No more.

Really. Fuck off. Don't push.

Exhausted…it'spointless.Ohto

Inhale fumes, release the tap.

Suffocating in my own hate.

REFLECTIONS

Why can't I see everything you say that I am
when you're trying your hardest to help me?

My eyes are shut, the lenses warped.
You hold up a mirror but all I see
is depression and weakness.

What is the truth? Both cannot be.
I want to believe, to see as you do.

But who am I?

Am I the reflection I see
in the mirror, or in your eyes?

STUBBORN YIELDING

Whack whack
Tickle attack
Lunge
Hug
Sob

You Were There

you were there
holding me close
as I rejected love
desiring death
and sufferings relief

you were there
on the phone
confessing love
as I vomited pills
and shook

you were there
through the night
declaring your love
keeping sleepless vigil
so I could rest

you were there
at the hospital
giving me strength love
bringing me home
to live and heal

you were there
and I am here
thanking you love
for all that then
and now

OUT

It's an odd sensation:
Sunlight reflecting off the tears
Caught in my eyelashes
As I coax Bertha
Slowly, slowly, up the hill
To the chaos that awaits me.

GREEN

My lover is as silent as the drizzle
that slides down the windshield.
I pretzel my legs and press my tongue
to the back of my teeth, hard.
His breath is thunderous, mocking.
In, out, in, out, in, nose whistling.

I punch his shoulder and leap out
strutting to the headstone
sunk into the grass among the upright plaques
he has locked the car and is picking dandelions
which grow between the cement and the gravel
disgusting bright dyes which
must be plucked every summer
only to return multiplied the next

I stomp atop the soil
and wave my arms ridiculously,
daring him to meet my eyes.
There's nothing sacred in this earth.
His horrified stare satisfies me
until he steps forward.

the weeds flop about in his too-slow hands
and he rests them on her grave
the trees rustle and echo the
bible verse read twice
the trees shall clap their hands

I spin and wander through
the questions in his eyes.
Through the Johnsons, Smiths, and Raymonts,
sneaking glances at his bowed head,
his careful touch smoothing the earth
and sweeping away the crinkled leaves.
How absurd; he mutters.
Speaking to rotting flesh encased in cedar
covered by green
as if she was ever there at all,
this woman he never met.

a wasp flutters by and I shout daring it to sting
but it is gone and he mutters as the trees rustle
and the grass blinds and as I collapse
under imagined pain
we drive away dry-eyed and joking
and I wonder if I ever screamed at all

QUALITY TIME

I Understand

I lie in the warm spot Dad left
When he was sent, grumbling, to the couch.
You curl your body around mine and
Run cool fingertips through the silence in my hair.
I want to explain my entrance
But can't so I tighten my lips together,
And we lie there together
Alone with our thoughts until I regret knocking.

"I would cry myself to sleep when I was your age.
I wept for the world and all the evil in it."
You whisper in my ear as tears pool on the fabric
Until they soak into the pillow.

The crickets, and frogs, in our pool, keep time,
As it slips, and slows, to meaning.
"I once asked God my worth through prayer
And dreamt all through the night I was
Flipping through checks, all written out to me."

I hear the promise through my silent suffering
Then sigh and hug you close
As we dream.

LEGEND

The family's all feasting,
but young Stephen can't sit still.
Slipping out of the chair,
he races to the adjacent bathroom.
Relieved, he streams, but the door didn't latch!
Father notices the door slowly swinging open,
and booms, "Hey Steve, how's it going in there?"
Dozens of amused eyes turn
to see the blushing boy.

ADVENTURES IN THE SANDBOX

Guess what!
Dad made me a present today.
He hammered four planks of wood
Into a rectangular storage bay.
He filled it with sand then went inside
And only came back out
When I cried, and cried, and cried.

"What's wrong?"
He called to me,
"Did you fall, are you hurt?"
As he ran out to see.

I had filled the sandbox with my toys,
Shiny Tonka trucks piled high.
It was so full I didn't fit!
That's why I cried.

GRATEFUL CURSING

A scared girl of fourteen,
I was worried 'bout my mom.
Three days she'd been in labor
And that's real long.
I got a call at school;
I had a brother at home.
I was a fool to worry,
"Both doing well," said the phone.
I met my little brother,
Counted fingers and toes.
Laughed, hugged,
You know how that goes.

He was a baby boy born of September,
A precious gift of love,
The only thanks I remember
Amongst cursing God above.

Days later Mom was still tired,
All her time spent in rest.
They didn't know what was wrong.
Our family tried our best.
Only six days after the birth
Our mother was taken.
We gave her body to the earth;
She would never awaken.

But we had our baby boy born of September,
A precious gift of love,
The only thanks I remember
Amongst cursing God above.

Now he's a boy of four:
Trucks, belches, and all.
But we'll miss our mom forever
'Cause the Lord made his call.
What did she think that night?
Did she wish she could say,
"Let me go into the sky.
Cry, scream, and pray?"

"Remember my baby boy born of September,
Holy precious gift of love,
This thanks be sure you remember
Even while cursing God above."

Could she be watching us now?
Does Mom feel the pain,
Or joy, or peace? I can't imagine.
Hateful thanks drives me insane.
That baby's still the only thanks that I remember
Amongst cursing God above.

FAITH

Thank you, God,
for the lessons
that today's pain will bring.
Thank you for
your confidence in me
and the promise
that you will never
give me more trials
than I can handle.

INSIDE

Grandma you left before I could ask you
to hold on. I had so much to say.
Now I can't cause you're gone.
But the world will keep on spinning
and soon I'll see that your love lives on
forever, inside of me.

Mommy you're gone. You left so suddenly.
You were my best friend but
you couldn't bring me.
The world will keep on spinning
and soon I'll see that your love lives on
forever, inside of me.

These women, my family,
a part of me they'll always be.
The world just keeps on spinning
and now I see that their love does live on
forever, inside of you and me.

ROCK A BUOY

There is a river

which flows

as my heart,

spilling out of itself

into others' lives

as they stream

into mine.

They connect

in swirling shades and hues:

angry cucumber, solemn

glitter, and wistful mango.

SPARKS

A word sparks a memory and I fade from reality,
appearing to stare intently at you as I journey back.

Smiling lips hid yellow-green teeth in photographs.
She bought four sessions of whitening but
Couldn't sleep through her pain that night
From the first day's procedure.
Dad was out on business so she shook me awake,
Tears dripping off her cheeks to dot my blankets.
Twelve years old, I knew I should help
But I was selfish and tired so I half-heartedly
Prayed with and sang to her, and soon fell asleep,
Leaving her to face that pain alone.

Her pained expression gives place to yours
And you ask if everything's okay.
Suddenly it isn't alright. With that one moment,
In that one thought, I am lost—
Acutely thrashing in a sea of guilt and self-hatred.
My body reacts and I ball up, shivering,
Wanting to take it all back.

THROUGH

Lover I pace at the door till two
As you romance Valentine new
I watch as you and what's her name
Come giggle waltzing down the lane
And my heart weeps at the heat of you

VENOM AND EGGS

She and he and she and they are there
But where am I?
Trampled on by the crowd,
I'm only the silence in the howl.

I have run out of venom and eggs
And will soon desert myself
Unless I can manage to kill them

By myself.

ELABORATE

I'm caught in the trap of what we're taught to
believe: the healing properties of chocolate
orgasms, taboo desires, and deviled eggs, and the
venomous me wanting out and in simultaneously.
Nothing is between carcass rot and twinkle alive.
They're separately joined in nude dressings; solid
invisibilities; transparent facts which milk truths until
nothing is real or right. Pause to ask which and the
moment is gone and, mockingly, no more appear.
Desires flare too quickly to take root. Their trunks
and branches itch flame and must be planked and
papered so suddenly, seeming to emerge from
cherished infant to thirty-eight in one moment. Fetal
wishes bruise poetry on seasoned flesh.

MUTED

Death, suicide, mutilation – these are child's words
likened to snowball, lemonade, and elf.
Drained of threats, they're just games.
Gain a hug, lover, liar, fraud, and drive him away.
Suck'em in to spit them out
farther than they would have traveled alone
unwounded, unscathed, unmuted.

Hang up and he'll call again.
Reel him in good and tight.
Tight like my bloodied cunt,
puffed and bruised from my fisted bite.
"Stop that; you're scaring me; pick up the phone!"
I only scare you when I try to, freaky fucked up girl.
You don't recognize, don't realize she's there
until I point and kick, scream, run, hang up.
Then you say, "It's okay, you'll get through it,
I'll help, talk to me." And though you try,
I remain muted.

I start spitting you, helper, failure, out farther.
And there's no escape, no escape until the next he,
whose heart I will tear and scratch
worse than my pussy, unless I get rid of her.
So I swallow twenty-one antimutation possibilities
and am wheeled to the hospital,
to the mental health clinic,
which gives me half a pill a day to control her
so I won't be muted.

But it is she who can withstand the attacks,
Not me
Tonight.

We Need to Talk

"We need to talk," the message simply said.
He slams the phone down and races to her room,
tripping over untied shoelaces.
Something in her voice, that desperation.
What happened, what did he do, is she okay?
Wringing questions as he sprints across campus.

Over there. There, under the multitude of covers.
She shivers, waiting, longing to be held
but that's what got her into this in the first place.

Flinging the door aside he kneels,
kissing the tears that are streaming down,
tasting their sweet saltiness.
She wonders how to begin.
He lifts her chin and she stares through him,
her crystal gaze magnifying the questions.
She shakes, splattering teardrops on his nose.

"I'm listening. What is it?"
She sighs and surrenders to his embrace,
weightless in the instant warmth.
"I'm pregnant."

MOTHER

She stands
There with her
Swollen feet, her
Aching back, her
Hot temperature
And knows
That
Her
Body lies.
These signs, the
So-called symptoms
Mask the majesty
The wondrous
Awe and
Peace that
She feels now
That she is never
Alone. God has given
Her something, a gift of
Love, who reaches out,
Grabs her heart... kicks,
Squirms within her and
She cannot conceal her
Excitement that
She
Will
Soon
See
Her
Daughter.

Why

Compose.

To: mary@email.com.

Subject: Why did you leave me?

Mom, I don't understand.
You were supposed to die after
you'd met your grandkids, your great-grandkids.
We need you. I need you.
I'm so confused. Why did you give up?

Was it me? Was it because I forgot
to say, "goodnight, I love you"?
Did I not pray hard enough, often enough,
well enough?

It's just not fair.
You won't be there at my sweet sixteen party,
graduation, when I get my braces off,
or to guide me when I get my first boyfriend.

I have nobody to talk to.
There are too many people that want to help
when they can't.
At school, strangers are saying,
"If you ever need to talk, I am here."
I don't want to talk to them.
They don't even know me, and
they don't know you.
They'll never understand.
I can't talk to anyone about this.

Mom, it's not fair to Estey, Jimmy, or Dad either.
Jimmy only knew you while he grew inside of you, plus a mere six days.
He won't even remember you
or know his mother's love.

Oh God. What if I don't remember you?
What if I forget the little things,
like how you loved green because of the trees
and how you sang hymns out of key.
Every year you would try again to make apple pie
and Dad would name the result "apple soup".
You called me Megs, and I might forget that.

 Of course, there are some things that I
want to forget... that I'm desperate to forget.
I don't want to remember my numbness
when the ambulance pulled into our driveway
just as my school bus drove me away.
And how it felt when I called home that day
and asked if I could stay after school
to do homework. I could not make myself say
the words: "Is everything ok? What is going on?
Why was there an ambulance? Can I talk to Mom?"
All I wanted to hear was that everything was ok.

But it's not ok. Nothing's ever going to be ok again.

Send.

Compose.

To: mary@email.com.

Subject: Goodbye.

I love you.

Send.

Close.

DRAIN

My spider plant is dying and I am going numb.
Your arms may dam the flood but
A single drop of blood and they flee,
Only to return me bound and helpless.

The numb dumb hatred, pink under the nails
Is weary of sleep and wake,
Surrendering moments of shame,
Hastily overturned and buried.

No more soul's hide-and-seek game.
I am only the mask; the pain, the past.

FORTRESS

thirst consumes
demons' fortress beneath
mustn't touch the ground
shivering under my little girl sheets
whimpering mommy
the waves topple
and angry clouds thunder
can't hear
door is open
dark shadow concealing dorothy
hostage of winged monkeys
growl in their bloodshot glow
nevermind

SLICED

sometimes in the night I surrender without a fight
condomless it penetrates multiplying my desire

only last night visions of mother's fight
rippled in every surface scalding my fury

this cursed night I don't want to fight
punctures polka dot organs sitting on the bible

JUST FOR SPITE

I'll serve you liver, definitely liver.
There's nothing grosser tasting,
Not even fried rooster's balls.
Maybe some sticky-slimy octopi
On the side with the ink still in them
So when you stick your fork in
They'll squirt you in the face.
You think you're okay on the drink:
Soda in an opaque glass.
But you reach the bottom quickly
And get a mouthful of drowned ants.

FREDERICK

How many terrorists have you
seen come through here tonight?
You know, the London problem?
Well, I just saw two.
Don't let any of this upset you though.

BUNNY FOR PRESIDENT

Vote Bunny. Vote today.
Vote Bunny. We want it her way!

Goodbye flags of red, white and blue,
Purple and green are the colors true.
Mannequins gone and bra ads too
So we'll all feel gorgeous, even you!

Vote Bunny. Vote today.
Vote Bunny. We want it her way!

No, no, this isn't a dream
Bunny is more fun than mainstream.
She will declare a new theme,
A national holiday for ice cream!

Vote Bunny. Vote today.
Vote Bunny. We want it her way!

DESSERT

Mary was supposed to have cooked.
They were waiting for oven-fresh treats.
Quickly she ripped open the package,
spread them on the tray, threw out the evidence.
Offering tall glasses of milk, she entertained
visitors with her recipe for freshly baked Oreo
cookies. "Be careful," she concluded with a wink,
"Don't burn yourself."

CELEBRATIONS

Lobster dinner
Cloth napkins
Salty sweet kisses
Confessions
Encircling arms squeezing tight
Safe
Warm

Key in
Engine sputters
Headlights on
Drift
In out
Into sleep
On the long, long ride home

The door creaks
Black heels tap tap
Click the light
Turn to kiss goodnight

SURPRISE
Heartpoundingohmygodican'tbreatheihateyouguys
Wide   awake

Happy birthday

CHOCOLATE OBSESSION

Ooooo ohhhh
Big bubbling beautiful
Slippery silky smooth
Eat everything eaten
Slowly steadily sweeter
Savoring salty sensations
Intimate icy image
Okay only one
Not 'nother Nestle

SAUSAGE

Trousers slipped down, Nathan's Sir
rose even nearer. Rachel let this
sweet torture
extend during girl's strip posing.
Giggles snap, pinch. "Hello."

STIGMA

Sweet sticky pollen sways and bumps
Tempting, luring you, promoting me.
Impatient, I point, then wink through the
Gentle sunrise glow and you, stumbling,
Make it to me. Sultry hummed scream of breeze
And we part, until you next desire honey.

SELF-PORTRAIT

SILENCE

The minutes would tick

                          but time's digital.

The mice would scurry

                          but poison eliminates.

The sky would fall

                          but the clouds are dry.

The electricity would click

                          but blankets warm.

The child would whimper

                          but dreams occupy.

The sheets would rustle

                          but I am still,

staring into the silence.

34 NOTHING

May I help you find something?
Unhuh, underwire, sexy, padded.
We have some great styles over here.
Do you like strapless?
Why don't you start with these.
The dressing room is right here.
I'll check on you in a few minutes.

How's it going?
Looks like that cup is too big.
What about the back closure?
Okay so a thirty-two would be too tight.
I'll be right back with some more options.

Ma'am? I'm back.
None of those fit?
Okay try these, they're a smaller cup size.

No, we don't carry anything smaller
than a double A.

Once Again

With the night

comes unbearable cold

and I tire prematurely.

I crawl beneath ten blankets

and still I shiver.

And so,

once again,

I stain your pillow with my tears

and wish you were in my arms.

SCENTED TASTE

And I'll wiggle my thumb slick with the slime
    until I can't taste where
    it came from anymore.

Your fervent plunging and twisting
    couldn't bring me
    to this humming silence.

And in that eternal moment
    this draftless void
    and her giggles are nothing.

Fainted Within

She mourned tender without blemish
as a cherub weeping snowflakes.
Sunlit darkness mirrored enthusiastic greeting.
Sparkled smile echoed in her tight mouth.

How's your mom?

She clung and swift was hewn down,
must admit death aloud.
Syllables bite and bruise fears validated well.

OH GOD

Bulging bulbous blossoms
Of orange-brown hue
Sweep September aside
And mount Autumn,
Breaking bread bareback.